Dear Parent:
Your child's love of reading starts here!

Every child learns to read in a different way and at his or her own speed. You can help your young reader improve and become more confident by encouraging his or her own interests and abilities. You can also guide your child's spiritual development by reading stories with biblical values and Bible stories, like I Can Read! books published by Zonderkidz. From books your child reads with you to the first books he or she reads alone, there are I Can Read! books for every stage of reading:

 SHARED READING
Basic language, word repetition, and whimsical illustrations, ideal for sharing with your emergent reader.

 BEGINNING READING
Short sentences, familiar words, and simple concepts for children eager to read on their own.

 READING WITH HELP
Engaging stories, longer sentences, and language play for developing readers.

 READING ALONE
Complex plots, challenging vocabulary, and high-interest topics for the independent reader.

 ADVANCED READING
Short paragraphs, chapters, and exciting themes for the perfect bridge to chapter books.

I Can Read! books have introduced children to the joy of reading since 1957. Featuring award-winning authors and illustrators and a fabulous cast of beloved characters, I Can Read! books set the standard for beginning readers.

A lifetime of discovery begins with the magical words **"I Can Read!"**

Visit www.icanread.com for information on enriching your child's reading experience.
Visit www.zonderkidz.com for more Zonderkidz I Can Read! titles.

Then God said, "Let the land produce plants."
—*Genesis 1:11 (NIrV)*

ZONDERKIDZ

Poisonous, Smelly, and Amazing Plants
Copyright © 2010 by Zonderkidz

Requests for information should be addressed to:
Zonderkidz, *Grand Rapids, Michigan 49530*

Library of Congress Cataloging-in-Publication Data
   Poisonous, smelly, and amazing plants.
      p. cm. — (I can read!)
    ISBN 978-0-310-72008-9 (softcover)
   1. Plants in the Bible—Juvenile literature.
   BS665.P65 2010
   231.7'65—dc22   2009054373

Editor: Mary Hassinger
Art direction & design: Sarah Molegraaf

Printed in China

---

10 11 12 13 14 /SCC/ 5 4 3 2 1

I Can Read!

· · · MADE · BY · GOD · · ·

Poisonous, Smelly, and Amazing Plants

CONTENTS

Some of the most special things

God made are called plants.

Some are poisonous,

some are smelly,

and some are just amazing.

One special plant God made

is a mushroom called the fly agaric.

It is one of over fourteen thousand

kinds of mushrooms.

The fly agaric grows mostly

in the northern half of the earth.

They can be found in other places too.

These mushrooms grow in groups.

The fly agaric is poisonous.

It will make you sick if you eat it!

God made sure the fly agaric

would be noticed.

He made them look like bright

red umbrellas with white polka dots.

The tops of these mushrooms are about three to eight inches around. If you spot one, try to stay away.

Another plant to stay away from

is very smelly.

It is called the corpse plant.

God made this plant smell

like rotten meat!

The flower is even red, like raw meat.

The terrible smell brings bugs
from miles away.
These bugs help the plant to grow
by pollinating it.

The corpse plant grows wild
in the rainforests of Sumatra.
Sumatra is an island north
of Australia.

It is also grown in special buildings
called greenhouses.

God made the corpse plant one of
the biggest flower buds in the world—
some are four feet across!
This flower can grow
up to six inches in one day.

Leaves on the corpse plant

can grow twelve feet tall!

That is as tall as the ceiling.

The Venus flytrap is another plant you might want to stay away from.

God made Venus flytraps

very special—they can bite!

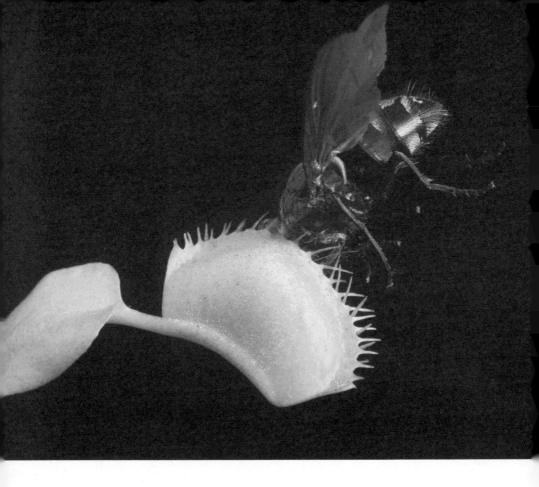

Venus flytraps eat bugs.

The tiny trap of the plant

has small hairs.

When something touches the hair,

the trap will close

in less than one second!

It can take up to ten days

for a Venus flytrap to eat one bug.

They love flies, spiders, and crickets.

Venus flytraps grow wild
in very few places—
mostly in swamps and other
humid places in North Carolina.
You can buy a Venus flytrap at a
flower nursery or store though.

The Venus flytrap grows

to be four to six inches tall.

Its trap is about an inch long.

There is usually one trap

for each leaf on the plant.

God made the Venus flytrap
small but very special.
He also created huge plants.
One of them is an amazing tree
called a redwood.

Redwood trees are mostly found

in northern California.

These are huge trees!

A redwood might grow 400 feet high,

and up to 20 feet around.

Redwood trees live a long time.

A redwood might live to be

2,000 years old!

Redwoods live long because the bark is thick and strong. It does not get hurt easily by fire or fungus.

Another huge tree is
the giant sequoia.
Many giant sequoia grow in
the Sierra Nevada mountains
in California.

The giant sequoia are shorter and

fatter than redwood trees.

They grow up to 300 feet high,

and up to 30 feet in diameter.

Some live 3,000 years or more.

General Sherman is the name
of the largest tree in the world.
It is a giant sequoia that is still
growing in California.
People think it is about
2,300 years old!

Another famous sequoia is

Tunnel Log in Sequoia National Park.

This tree fell across a road.

It is so big that people

made a tunnel in it.

You can drive a car through it.

God made plants all around us.
God's plan is that we keep
plants healthy and growing.
Plants help us to stay
healthy and grow too!